DISCOVER

The Yorkshire Coast & Moors

John Potter

CONTENTS

▲▲ **Scarborough** Sunrise over South Bay looking towards Filey in the distance.
▲ **Sutton Bank** One of the finest views in the north of England is from Sutton Bank over the Vale of York and Mowbray towards the Yorkshire Dales.

MYRIAD

The Heritage Coast

The eastern boundary of the North York Moors National Park is known as the North Yorkshire Heritage Coast. This is a beautiful and varied landscape with high rugged cliffs, traditional fishing villages, small river inlets and wide sandy bays. The Heritage Coast includes the resorts of Sandsend, Runswick Bay, Whitby, Robin Hood's Bay and Ravenscar. The Cleveland Way National Trail runs the entire length of this coastline and provides exhilarating walks along the cliffs at Whitby and Ravenscar.

Sandsend This pretty fishing village is located at the foot of Lythe Bank where the sandy beach comes to an abrupt end. There are many picturesque cottages set against a backdrop of cliffs beside two meandering streams which flow out onto the beach.

◀ **Staithes** Beloved of artists and photographers, the quaint village of Staithes is in a dramatic setting on the rugged stretch of coast north of Whitby.

▼ **Runswick Bay** Situated at the foot of cliffs between Staithes and Sandsend, Runswick Bay oozes charm. With its maze of narrow winding alleys and cobbled paths weaving their way through tiny cottages, it is easy to imagine you are back in a seafaring landscape many centuries ago.

WHITBY

▲ **The town** Often referred to as "Captain Cook's country", the seaside town of Whitby and its surrounding countryside, where the young James Cook learned the seafarer's trade, is steeped in maritime history. The house in Grape Lane where he served his apprenticeship is now a museum. The 199 steps that connect the parish church of St Mary to the town are a local institution. These "church stairs" were used to carry coffins up to the church; there are resting places for the pall-bearers along the way.

▼ **St Hilda's Abbey** Whitby's skyline is dominated by the ruins of St Hilda's Abbey, high up on East Cliff. The nearby parish church of St Mary is one of the finest Anglo-Saxon churches in the north of England. The quaint winding streets in the town below are lined with galleries, cafes, craft shops and tearooms.

▲ **The harbour** Whitby has the only natural harbour between the river Tees and the Humber. The photographer Frank Meadows Sutcliffe immortalised the town and the life of its fishing community in scores of beautiful sepia-tinted photographs, many of which can be seen in the Sutcliffe Gallery in the town. The author Bram Stoker set much of his classic Victorian novel *Dracula* in and around the town and today visitors with a taste for the Gothic can take the Dracula Trail Tour.

ROBIN HOOD'S BAY

▶▼ **Historic town** South of Whitby, this picturesque fishing village has a series of steep winding streets and narrow alleyways (ginnels) lined with old houses and cottages, many with distinctive red pantiled roofs. In the 18th century the bay was a centre for smuggling and there are a number of secret tunnels below the houses.

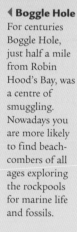

◀ Boggle Hole
For centuries Boggle Hole, just half a mile from Robin Hood's Bay, was a centre of smuggling. Nowadays you are more likely to find beach-combers of all ages exploring the rockpools for marine life and fossils.

▲ ▼ Ravenscar One of the wildest and most exposed places on the Yorkshire coast, the cliffs at Ravenscar are almost 600ft above sea level. The headland is now owned by the National Trust and there are fabulous views of Robin Hood's Bay from the coastal clifftop path, part of the Cleveland Way.

The Sunshine Coast

The long established holiday resorts of Scarborough, Filey, Bridlington, Hornsea and Withernsea are blessed with glorious sandy beaches and their location on the east coast gives them maximum hours of sunshine. Scarborough developed as Britain's first seaside resort in the early 19th century, followed by Bridlington – the two towns competing to be the premier centre of sun, sand and seaside entertainment for holidaymakers from all over the north of England.

◄ Cromer Point Just north of Scarborough, close to the village of Burniston, there are tremendous views of Scarborough Castle from the headland at Cromer Point. The rockpools below the cliffs are particularly dramatic at first light.

▲▼ Scarborough
The ruined Norman castle and its headland dominate Scarborough's skyline, dividing the town into North and South Bay. One of the best views of the town and headland is from St Oliver's Mount, just above the spa complex with its superb parks, gardens, theatres and conference hall. Overlooking the South Bay is the Grand Hotel; completed in 1867, at the time it was one of the largest hotels in the world. Its four towers represented the seasons and its 12 floors the months of the year.

FILEY & BEMPTON

▲ **The beach** Filey is an elegant and unspoilt seaside town. The five-mile sandy beach is protected from the north by Filey Brigg, a finger of gritstone which projects one mile into the sea forming a natural pier and breakwater. In a superb position looking out over the bay, Filey was transformed from a small fishing village into a "planned" town in the early 19th century. This small and friendly resort has many attractions including Coble Landing, where fishing boats rest at jaunty angles outside the popular beachside cafes. The town stages a week-long Edwardian festival every June and many local people dress up in period costume.

Bempton Cliffs At the southern end of Filey Bay, Bempton has some of the highest cliffs on the east coast of Britain. The RSPB bought the cliffs in 1969 and Bempton is now one of the most famous nature reserves for seabirds in the UK. Puffin, guillemot and kittiwake abound on the cliffs; a major attraction is the huge gannet colony – the only nesting site for these birds, Britain's largest seabird, on the mainland. Access for visitors is easy by car or on foot from the little village of Bempton, one mile inland.

FLAMBOROUGH TO HORNSEA

▲ Flamborough Head The coastline at Flamborough Head is one of the most spectacular areas of chalk cliff in Britain. Dramatic cliffs, some reaching 400ft, thrust into the sea, providing a haven for birdlife. Thornwick Bay is just one of the many sheltered, shingle coves fronting the sea with caves and dramatic stacks. The old beacon lighthouse at Flamborough was first built in 1669 but there is no evidence that it was ever used. The "new" lighthouse was built in 1806 by John Matson of Bridlington.

▶ Sewerby This tiny hamlet stands on the coast just two miles north of Bridlington. The photograph looks towards Bridlington and shows the dramatic coastal erosion along the beach.

▲ Bridlington Sandy beaches, elegant promenades and a bustling harbour provide all the essential holiday ingredients. From the north pier and beach Flamborough Head and lighthouse are visible. Recently, the large fishing fleet has given way to yachts and pleasurecraft.

▼ Hornsea Situated between Hull and Bridlington, this little resort has a long shingle beach and spectacular views towards Spurn Head and the Humber estuary. Hornsea's best-known attraction is its Mere, the largest freshwater lake in Yorkshire.

WITHERNSEA TO HULL

▶ **Withernsea** The lighthouse stands in the middle of the town – a sign that local people were concerned about coastal erosion centuries ago. Climb the 144 steps to the lamproom at the top and there are breathtaking views of the town and surrounding countryside.

▼ **Spurn Head** Situated on the north bank of the entrance to the river Humber, this three-mile long finger of land that snakes out into the Humber estuary is constantly being reshaped by storms and coastal erosion. Spurn is an important feeding and stopping-off point for thousands of migrating birds. The distinctive black-and-white Spurn Point lighthouse became redundant in 1985 and has now been replaced by automatic beacons. Since 1810 the Humber lifeboat has been stationed at Spurn Point; the crew of seven men and their families live in houses close to the station.

Humber Bridge Opened in 1981, this beautiful suspension bridge was built to link north Lincolnshire and Humberside across the wide Humber estuary. Almost 1.5 miles long, the bridge has cut 50 miles off the road journey between the major ports of Hull and Grimsby.

▲**The Deep** The gleaming glass and aluminium marine life centre opened in 2002. Standing at the confluence of the rivers Hull and Humber this unique visitor attraction was designed by the architect Sir Terry Farrell.

◀ **Hull** The Humber and Railway Dock in the centre of the city was once part of a large complex which housed the city's whaling and deep sea fishing fleet. Now the dock is part of the Hull Marina complex, constructed in 1983. The large black vessel is the old Spurn Lightship which was previously moored east of Spurn Point. Built in 1927 it has been restored and guided tours are available.

Northern Moors

This is a region where it is possible to unwind and enjoy some of the finest scenery in Britain. In the west the remote heather-clad moors of the Cleveland Hills gradually give way to the lush green valley of the Esk with its pretty villages of Westerdale, Castleton, Danby and Glaisdale. For a different perspective, travel on a steam train on the North York Moors Railway which links the *Heartbeat* village of Goathland, Levisham with its beautiful forest walks and Grosmont with its superbly restored railway station.

▲ **Castleton** Situated
in the Upper Esk valley,
Castleton sits proudly on
a high ridge where the lush
green valleys of Westerdale
and Danby Dale come
together. This wintry view
of the village was taken from
Castleton Rigg, looking
north-east towards Danby
Park Wood and Haw Rigg.

◀ **Westerdale** Young
Ralph Cross marks the point
where the minor road into
Westerdale joins the Hutton-
le-Hole to Castleton road
at Rosedale Head. The cross
was erected in memory of
a destitute traveller who
perished from exhaustion
in this remote spot.

GLAISDALE TO DANBY

▲ **Fryup Dale** This quaintly named corner of North Yorkshire consists of two secluded valleys, Great and Little Fryup, which wind off the Esk valley. A scattering of farms and cottages are surrounded by magnificent purple heather-clad moors with trails and walks across the moorland. This is an ideal place from which to explore *Heartbeat* country.

▶ **Glaisdale** The valley around Glaisdale is truly majestic when seen in winter from high up on the fell. The area once had an abundance of iron ore and, in the 19th century, there were three blast furnaces in the valley.

Danby Nestling in a hollow at the western end of the beautiful Esk valley this little settlement has a ruined castle and working water-mill. Scottish Blackface sheep graze on the large green in the centre of the village. The Danby Show, which takes place every August, is a popular event for the local farming community and many visitors flock to the village to soak up the atmosphere, admire the livestock and enjoy the traditional events.

Roseberry Topping On the border between the North York Moors and Cleveland, the distinctive half-cone shape of Roseberry Topping dominates much of the countryside around Guisborough. The hill's peculiar shape is due to the fact that half the summit has collapsed, due either to a geological fault or to the many old alum and ironstone mines close to the top.

LITTLE BECK

Falling Foss waterfall
Located close to the tiny
hamlet of Little Beck,
which stands on a tribu-
tary of the river Esk, this
beautiful waterfall can be
reached via a pleasant
woodland walk through
Little Beck and May Beck
Wood towards the head of
the valley. The waterfall
tumbles down a 30ft deep
gorge and is spectacular,
particularly after heavy
rainfall.

Mallyan Spout The highest waterfall on the North York Moors, Mallyan Spout, near Goathland, cascades 60ft down the side of West Beck Gorge. A short walk alongside the beck just to the right of the Mallyan Spout Hotel leads to the waterfall; in wet weather spray is blown across the path so that visitors have the impression of walking through the waterfall.

▶▶ **Goathland** The parish church of St Mary stands at the centre of this beautiful village. Goathland lies on the 24-mile North York Moors railway, from Pickering to Grosmont.

▶ **Grosmont** Morris men perform on the platform of the beautifully restored Grosmont station. This is the northern terminus of the railway and connects with the Esk Valley railway. The village owes its existence to the railway; brickworks, limekilns and blast furnaces once clustered around the railhead.

Southern Moors

This region is dominated by a series of dales which run directly north into the heart of the North York Moors – Rosedale, Farndale, Bransdale, Ryedale and Bilsdale. As you head up each dale, the landscape changes from lush pastureland to open moorland and you pass through a number of pretty villages which help give each dale its own distinct character. To the west lies the beautiful Rievaulx Abbey and beyond the Hambleton Hills and Sutton Bank with its breathtaking views to the Yorkshire Dales.

◀ **Cropton Forest**
To the north of Cropton, the forest has a campsite, log cabins and outdoor activity centres. The area was cast as the forbidden forest in the *Harry Potter* films.

▶ **Cropton** This pretty village has a restored well, a reminder of a bygone era before piped water was introduced to the village in the 1920s. The 200-year-old New Inn is at the heart of village life and runs its own brewery.

▲ Rosedale
This long extend-
ed valley stretches
south-east from
Westerdale Moor
and Danby High Moor towards Hartoft End and
Cropton Forest. The river Seven flows the length of
the valley.

◀ Rosedale Abbey Despite its name, this pretty
village was never the site of an abbey.
The church of St Lawrence is at its centre and, close
by, is the Abbey Store and Tea Room which houses a
national park information centre. The popular
Rosedale Show takes place each August.

BILSDALE TO FARNDALE

▲ **Blakey Ridge** Part of the famous coast-to-coast trail, from St Bees in Cumbria to Robin Hood's Bay, the 24-mile stretch from Claybank over Blakey Ridge and then onto Grosmont traverses remote and mostly uninhabited moorland. Along the way there are a number of dramatic Bronze Age burial mounds and standing stones.

◀ **Bilsdale** The village of Fangdale Beck lies at the heart of Bilsdale, between West Moor and East Moor. There are many excellent walks up and over the moors from this sleepy hamlet; many would say that the area has some of the finest scenery in the north of England. Bilsdale has one of the oldest buildings on the North York Moors, the Old Sun Inn, also known as the Spout House.

◀▲▶ **Farndale** The tiny and picturesque hamlet of Church Houses nestles between the mighty Rudland Rigg and Blakey Ridge in glorious scenery at the heart of this much-loved dale. Best-known for its wild daffodils in spring, Farndale attracts up to 40,000 visitors each April. The daffodil walk follows the valley bottom beside the river Dove from Low Mill to Church Houses, passing the welcoming Feversham Arms. Pictured here is Church Houses and the winding road leading up to Blakey Ridge. The photograph was taken from Daleside Road at the foot of Horn Ridge.

HELMSLEY TO OLD BYLAND

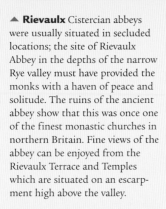

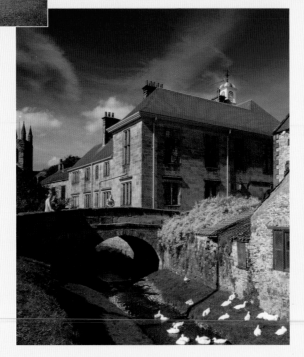

▲ **Rievaulx** Cistercian abbeys were usually situated in secluded locations; the site of Rievaulx Abbey in the depths of the narrow Rye valley must have provided the monks with a haven of peace and solitude. The ruins of the ancient abbey show that this was once one of the finest monastic churches in northern Britain. Fine views of the abbey can be enjoyed from the Rievaulx Terrace and Temples which are situated on an escarpment high above the valley.

▶ **Helmsley** One of the prettiest country towns in north Yorkshire, Helmsley is on the Thirsk to Scarborough road; it is an ideal centre for touring the area. The market square, complete with a stone arch bridge, is surrounded by fine mellow stone buildings.

◀▲ **Old Byland** Just west of Rievaulx, these cottages are clustered around the church of All Saints. In 1322 the Scots defeated the English at the Battle of Old Byland after Edward II had taken up residence in Rievaulx Abbey.

◀▲ **Hawnby** Set in the Hambleton Hills in Upper Ryedale, Hawnby is a remote village north of Rievaulx. The pretty parish church of All Saints stands some distance from the village, which is in two distinct halves. The split goes back to the mid 18th century when two local men, Chapman and Cornforth, experienced vivid dreams of God speaking to them. After meeting the preacher John Wesley they became the first Methodists in the neighbourhood. The village was owned by Lord Tancred, a devout Anglican, who was opposed to their cause. After being expelled from Hawnby, the two men settled in the lower part of the village where one of the first Methodist communities was established.

HUTTON-LE-HOLE

▲ **Hutton-le-Hole** One of the most popular stopping-off points for visitors to the North York Moors, Hutton's broad village green, dotted with moorland sheep, is an ideal spot for a summer picnic. The Ryedale Folk Museum, Yorkshire's leading open-air museum, has historic buildings depicting the daily life of North Yorkshire people from the earliest inhabitants up to the 1950s.

▶ **Gillamoor** This pretty village lies north of Kirkbymoorside on the minor road that links Fadmoor to Hutton-le-Hole. The village is well-known for its surprise view at the eastern end of the hamlet close to St Aidan's church. The view of Lower Farndale from this point is memorable whatever the season.

▲ **Lastingham** A peaceful haven nestling comfortably amidst glorious scenery, this is the ideal place to stroll and relax. The area around Lastingham has much to offer, with attractions such as Eden Camp Modern History Museum near Malton, the Flamingo Land theme park and Hutton-le-Hole folk museum.

▼ **Kirkbymoorside** A sizeable market town on the Helmsley to Pickering road, Kirkbymoorside is considered by many to be the gateway to the North York Moors. All Saints church is set back from the main street and lies next to an attractive landscaped area on the edge of town.

▲ **Hole of Horcum** Hollowed out of the heather-clad moor beside the Pickering to Whitby road, the Hole of Horcum is a huge natural amphi-theatre. Legend has it that "the devil's punchbowl", as it is known locally, was created by a giant named Wade who scooped out the rocks and earth, tossing them two miles east to Blakey Topping. A popular circular walk from the roadside car park passes this derelict farm cottage at Low Horcum.

◀▶ **Levisham** An attractive stop on the North York Moors railway, Levisham nestles above the quiet and wooded winding valley of Newton Dale, seven miles north of Pickering. The small church of St John the Baptist lies at the top of the village where the road and a footpath lead to the railway station in the bottom of the valley.

Pickering This busy and elegant market town is located on the southern edge of the North York Moors. In the town centre is Beck Isle Museum of Rural Life, housed in a listed Regency mansion. The museum transports visitors back through time as they pass through a wide variety of recreated settings including a cobblers shop, blacksmiths, chemists' shop, dairy and village store. The church of St Peter and St Paul has some rare medieval paintings uncovered in the 19th century. A major annual event is the Pickering traction engine rally, held on the showground.

▼ **Thornton-le-Dale** Just east of Pickering this little village has gift shops, tearooms and a sparkling stream. The small village green, with its ancient market cross and stocks, is surrounded by pretty cottages. This one is a favourite with photographers.

Sutton Bank The Hambleton Escarpment rises abruptly to a height of around 1000ft, giving views of more than 30 miles. Roulston Scar and Hood Hill lie to the left; Gormire Lake is lit by a dramatic sky stirred up by strong winds sweeping across the Vale of York. Just beyond Roulston Scar lies the White Horse of Kilburn, the well-known landmark created by local schoolmaster John Hodgson and his pupils in 1857.

Boltby Nestling in a deep narrow valley just west of the Hambleton Hills and two miles north of Gormire Lake, Boltby is a quiet and peaceful village whose main street is lined with attractive stone and brick cottages.

◀ **The Cleveland Way** A short walk along the escarpment brings you to Whitestone Cliff on the Cleveland Way footpath. The view here looks north towards Gormire Lake and Boltby. The 110-mile long Cleveland Way starts in the market town of Helmsley and traverses the upland ridge on the edge of the North York Moors, before reaching the coast at Saltburn-by-the-Sea. For its last 50 miles it continues along the coast, ending at Filey.